T0374028

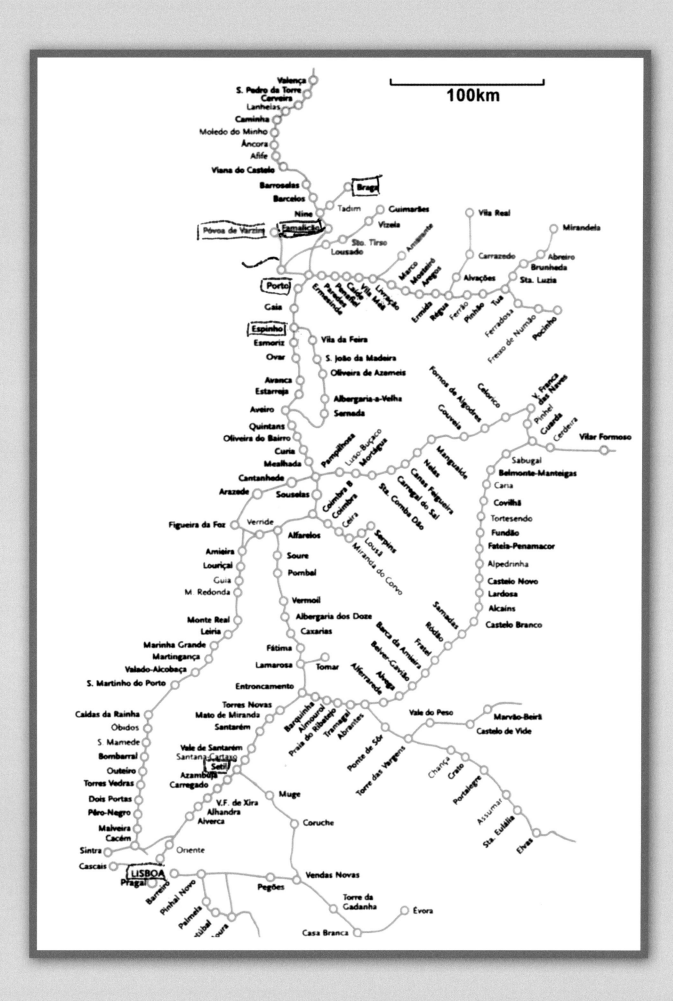

IBERIAN RAIL 1963:
The Atlantic Coast
by Fred Matthews

To order additional copies of this book, contact:
Xlibris
1-888-795-4274
www.Xlibris.com
Orders@Xlibris.com

Introduction:

This is the third volume recording an extensive tour of the railways and tramways of Iberia, made in the summer of 1963, when the traditional rail networks and motive-power had changed little. Because we recorded that rich and varied rail universe in color, which appears to be rare from that period, it seems worth while to leave this account.

This volume covers Portugal and the Galician seaport of Vigo, in northwestern Spain, with its little-known but striking tramway system. Aside from the publications by J.H. Price, D.W. Winkworth and W.J.K Davies mentioned in the text, a valuable source on Portugese railways just at the time of our visit is the detailed study by C.P. Boocock and A. Trichett, "The Railways of Portugal," in Railway World, August and September 1963.

Once again I should record my gratitude to the old friend with whom I made the pilgrimage, Larry Veysey, who desperately desired a summer's break from the academic world after several years' hard labor on the book that would soon establish his reputation, The Emergence of the American University.

This book is dedicated to the memory of
Laurence Russ Veysey 1932-2004
Distinguished Historian, Rail Enthusiast,
Stormy Petrel.

Title page: Vigo Bay, Bayona train

Rare bird: one of Lisbon's last (relatively) unaltered U.S. cars, built by St. Louis in 1909, heading for Belém via the inland route that paralleled the riverside 15. In the background is a heavily-rebuilt 340 series car originally produced by Brill in 1906. At the riverside Praça do Comércio.

Chapter 1: <u>TRAMWAY UTOPIA: LISBON AND SINTRA.</u>

After an overnight journey from the vast iron shed at Madrid Delicias, the vintage wagons-lits of the <u>Lusitania Express</u> deposited us mid-morning at Santa Apolonia, Lisbon's modest long-distance station, located a short tram ride up the Tagus from the historic centre. Our hotel was in the centre, the flat Baixa, the homogeneous 18th Century area rebuilt by the Marquis de Pombal in neoclassical style after the 1756 earthquake that destroyed most of the city. We were near Rossio, the central square, which had been a tram centre but by now had service only in the evenings, when the intrusion of yellow trams offered less obstruction to Lisbon's burgeoning motor traffic.

The Rossio cutback was part of a recent reorganization of service to dovetail with the first Metro line, city-owned, from the Baixa to Sete Rios. Except for clearing trams from the ceremonial Avenida da Liberdade north of the centre, the service reorganization did not entail a major decline in operation for the brilliantly-colored, sparklingly-clean trams, which still whirred and hissed over some 37 distinct routes laid to 90cm (2ft 11 7/16") gauge. With many turnback services and partial duplications, track mileage was not gigantic, about 90 according to J.H. Price's <u>Tramways of Portugal</u>, with 405 motor and 100 trailer cars available for service. Price noted also the superb condition of the cars, gleaming in the yellow and white that reflected the colors of brightly-clean Lisbon; and the American-style trolley poles with wheels, which created a nostalgic hissing as loud as the rather quiet motors. Overall, with its hills, narrow streets, and trams on all sides, Lisbon was a cleaner, brighter version of San Francisco in the 1940s.

The tramway was operated by the British-owned Companhia de Carris de Ferro de Lisboa, which electrified and expanded a horsecar system from 1900 to 1914, with a few extensions later. Perhaps because G.E. developed extra-narrow motors for the narrow cars, the first few hundred cars were built in the U.S., most by Brill, and shipped disassembled. After 1920 cars were built in the Carris' Santo Amaro shops, at first to Brill patterns but later with arch roofs and (after 1945) even boxy little streamliners. Because some major routes were fairly flat, but others featured 9% grades from the Baixa into the surrounding hills, there were two car types: with 25hp motors for "flat-line" routes and 45hp, plus "run-back" controllers for safety, for hill cars. Many cars had been rebodied over the years, but some of the oldest remained, relatively unaltered.

Just above Cais do Sodre, the inland routes to Belém and Boa Hora, the 14-16-17-19, running on Rua de São Paulo, passed under the bridge on Rua do Alecrim which carried the 20,29,31, and 30/32 circular. An even more traditional vehicle delays the inbound tram.

Truly a tramway city: three blocks above the Rua de São Paulo, at the Praça Luis de Camões,
a 20 to Cais do Sodré crosses the tracks of the 28 to Estrela and Prazeres Cemetery.
The inbound 28 track has curved around the Praça.

Original car: one of a handful of largely-unmodernized St. Louis cars from 1909, enclosed for winter
service, descending Rua do Alecrim from Praça Camões, with the duke's statue marking Cais do Sodré. 5

A circular-route tram pauses on Rua de San Pedro do Alcantara, at the top of the Gloria funicular which connects the Chiado hill with the Praça dos Restauradores, near the Rossio Square.

The 16ᵗʰ Century Mosteiro (Monastery) do Jerónimos, with another rare American survivor, Brill semi-convertible #501 of 1914, heading to the Baixa..

Our exploration of the vast system was time-limited, and ironically centred on those routes, either spectacular or serving tourist sites, that proved survivors into the early 21st Century. The natural starting point for exploring the Carris network was the monumental and spacious Praça do Comércio, where the Baixa fronted the River Tagus. Usually called Terreiro do Paço (Palace Square) by locals, the Praça is too large in relation to its surrounding structures (18th Century palaces now full of government offices) to form a satisfying, unified space. But it was a wonderful spot to watch people, and trams, and had plenty of history—the King and Crown Prince of Portugal were murdered here in 1908.

About eight short blocks west along the Rua do Arsenal was the Baixa's other anchor, the Praça Duque de Terciera, known locally as the Cais do Sodré. Here tram routes circled a giant statue of the Duke, with the suburban railway terminal for Estoril and Cascais just to the west. The steeply-graded Rua do Alecrim headed up into the Bairro Alto, the hills west of the Baixa, crossing above a narrow street that carried a group of routes paralleling the main riverside 15 west to Belém and beyond. This area of narrow streets and shops, both traditional and upscale, was one of the loveliest parts of the Lisbon tramway, though less known than the celebrated Graça Loop on the opposite side of the Baixa. Six or eight blocks up from Cais do Sodré, Rua do Alecrim changed its name twice before passing the top station of one of Lisbon's photogenic street-funiculars, the Gloria ascençor.

Given its frequent service and varied double-truck rolling stock, plus the major historic sites en route, we naturally focused on the long Route 15, which headed out to the grand Renaissance monastery at Belém, and then on for some distance into wealthy turn-of-century suburbs, Dafundo and Cruz Quedabra. Belém's great monastery was also served, at much higher speed, by the Estoril Railway's stainless-steel trains, which featured railfan seats like my recently-lost Key System in California.

From the Torre de Belém: an Estorial Railway train powered by an electric baggage car at bottom left, with a tram on route 15 in the centre, inland.

Posh suburb: Cruz Quedabra, at the west end of the riverside 15 line, with a recently-rebodied 343 class Brill car, originally built in 1906 for first-class service, heading inbound for Comércio.

Splendid survivor: a Brill car of 1909 (rebuilt 1927) in a procession headed for the Graça loop, near Praça da Figueira.

#704 on route 28 at the tightest passage on the Graça loop, with ice-cream vendor.

An old St. Louis-built 400, delayed by an important Lisbon ritual, the high-pressure cleaning of streets and walls that kept the city light and bright. The connection to Route 12 is visible at our feet.

The most spectacular, and already famous, sector of the <u>Carris</u> network was the Graça Loop, with its little connecting 12 line from Martim Moniz north of the Baixa. This loop made a large circuit of the old Alfama, the steep castle-topped hill just east of the Baixa, and then circled farther northeast into the Graça, the next hill beyond, a much newer area, built up in the late 19th and early 20th Centuries as a traditional hillside working-class area. Three routes served Graça; the 10 and 11 made the entire loop, traversing the Baixa before heading uphill from opposite ends of the flat centre. Route 28, from the parliament-buildings in Estrela west of the Baixa, ascended with the 10, turning back about two-thirds around the loop. The most spectacular part of the loop was just beyond the Praça São Tomé, where the short 12 line connected, and the loop made a sharp double reverse into very narrow streets where hand-signalmen sat in doorways to control traffic on single-track sections. The Graça loop surpassed the cable cars of Nob and Russian Hills in San Francisco in sheer urban fascination. It is remarkable, and satisfying, that the loop has survived many obstacles into the 21st Century.

A short ride west from Lisbon's Rossio station, at the north end of the Baixa, was that ultimate city-in-a-forest, Sintra, scattered over hills and valleys. Known for its fantastic 19th Century palaces, Sintra had a special attraction for railfans. This was the Companhia Sintra-Atlantico, an unchanged early-20th Century metre-gauge rural tramway that ran from Sintra station for eight miles, down onto the coastal plain and out to the tiny beach resort of Praia das Maçãs (Apple Beach). This truly splendid survivor was now running only from July through October, the high tourist season. Though still operated by the private company, it was subsidized by the town of Sintra, aware of its tourist value, and perhaps also worried by buses in high season on the narrow roads that paralleled the tracks.

The Sintra-Atlantico ran with its original cars, built in 1903 by Brill in Philadelphia and shipped disassembled. Three of the four closed motor cars had been rebuilt in Sintra to a Lisbon arch-roofed design—the rebuilding being done by Lisbon shopmen. There were also three closed and five open cross-bench trailers, plus three cross-bench motors on which passengers could ride next to the motorman. The large hand brakes were supplemented by rheostatic brakes.

The line was pleasantly rural rather than spectacularly scenic, except for the steep roadside descent from Sintra which gave glimpses of the hills and castles from below. One traditional bit of business was running-around the open trailer at Praia das Maçãs, where a grade allowed the motor to pull ahead, letting the trailer run around it into the terminal stub, guided by a <u>servente</u> (trolley-boy). The S.A. was far from speedy, but certainly one of the most relaxing rail trips I can recall. It's good to know that (except for the street-running stretch near the C.P. station) it has reopened, and seems likely to survive.

Two Sintra Atlantico trains at the stub-end terminus at Sintra's C.P. railway station.
#8 is a trailer built by Brill in 1903; one of the motors is a rebuilt closed car,
the other a classic Brill open-bench unit.

One of the Brill cross-bench motors, with passengers sitting beside the motorman,
battles traffic in Sintra's business centre while inbound to the C.P. station.
This congested section through Sintra did not survive.

Open-bench Brill motor #1 of 1903, the line's first car,
descends the twisty road leaving Sintra for the coastal plain below.

Vintage vehicles rule the road: one of the closed motor cars,
rebodied by Lisbon shopmen in the 1920s in Lisbon style, labors up the grade into Sintra.

Changing ends at Praia das Maçãs (Apple Beach), after the motor
had let the trailer drift into the siding, then backed to couple up.

Proud *servente*: the
trolley-boy completes the
shunting in front of the little
SA station. It was a fun job
in a stagnant economy.

Chapter 2: On the Broad Gauge

After several busy days in Lisbon, we embarked on the Foguete, the express Fiat railcar set from Lisbon Santa Apolonia to Porto São Bento. This is Portugal's main trunk route, completed in 1864 by the Royal Portugese Railway, except for Gustave Eiffel's celebrated Maria Pia bridge over the Douro (1877). In Portugal's first major main-line electrification project, it was being wired at 25KV A.C. By 1963 the electrification was in use about half-way north; and work was proceeding. We passed at least one steam-powered wire train. Other steam locos were prominent along the way, since connecting branches were not wired, and steam still took over for the north end of the main line. Setil, junction with the only connecting line to the system south of the Tagus, was a treasure-house of rare locos off inter-regional freight trains. The Setil-Vendas Nuevas line, largely for freight, had one of Portugal's first C.T.C installations.

The Lisbon-Porto line was more interesting for railway sights than for scenery or architectural interest. Railways try to find low grades, and until the 17th Century at least, towns were built on hills for defense. But the railway interest was top-notch, above all a big art-nouveau-styled 4-6-0, built in 1913 in Germany to a famous French design, that was heading a train for the Spanish border at the junction of Pampilhosa.

With the single exception of the profitable suburban electric line from Lisbon to Estoril and Cascais, all Portugese rail services were operated from the late 1920s by "CP" or "C.P.", more formally the Companhia dos Caminhos de Ferro Portugese, a nominally private company with extensive government supervision (and subsidy when government wished). CP operated over 2219 route miles; about three-quarters on the broad Iberian 5'6", the other 475 miles metre-gauge. As of 1962 there were 439 steam locos, with no less than 19 wheel arrangements on the broad gauge and seven among the 70 narrow-gauge locos, including 0-4-4-0 and 2-4-6-0 tank engines. (An excellent brief guide to CP history, and motive power as in 1966, is D.W. Winkworth's Railway Holiday in Portugal (David and Charles, 1968).

And there was great variety within wheel-arrangements—there were several different types of 0-6-0s, built between 1863 and 1928, and a variety of 4-6-0s dating from 1898 to 1940 (a rebuild). As in Spain, ancient 0-6-0s could be found simmering, and occasionally switching, around freight yards; but they also pushed passenger trains on the steep climb out of Porto's São Bento station, and even hauled local commuter trains. At the other end of the age spectrum, there were Alco 2-8-2s of 1944/5 and a few Spanish-built 4-8-0s from 1947. But Portugal had embraced diesels earlier than Spain; there were no orders for steam after 1950, and 64 diesel locos were operating by 1963 (mostly south of Lisbon), with another 86 added by 1968. Steam lingered on into the 1970s, with some operation on the metre gauge into the Eighties.

CP relied heavily on motive power from Germany, even before 1920 when it began to receive German locos as war reparations (Portugal had sent troops to the Western front.). Unlike Spain, which developed a major loco-building industry after 1915, Portugal never did. Perhaps the small home market was decisive, but the Salazar government's fear of the social effects of industrialization may also have played a role.

A striking trait of C.P. locomotives was their usual sparkling cleanliness. The C.P. was probably the last European railway to turn out locos all shined and gleaming. This may well have been a function of Portugal's relative poverty and high unemployment—a state-controlled company hired excess workers at low wages, and used them to help present a positive image. Whatever the reason, CP power was a joy to observe. As was travel on Portugese trains—clean, well-maintained and briskly-operated. V. S. Pritchett claimed that Portugese trains "must be the worst in the world," but we found them mostly faster and in better condition than the Spanish average. Of course, Portugal had avoided the ruinous Civil War that was only 23 years past on our visit.

*Edwardian station, Edwardian train: the Northern Express to Vigo in Spain
ready to leave Porto São Bento. It could have been 1913, when the high-drivered
ten wheeler was new, and the station itself less than a decade old..*

The heaviest, most powerful and certainly most impressive of CP's many broad-gauge ten-wheelers—a Henschel 4-cylinder machine of 1910-12 at Pampilhosa, on a local to the Spanish border. The design came from France's Chemin de Fer du Nord.

Expresses new and old: CP's morning <u>Foguete</u> to Porto, with three Fiat railcars, next to 1920s Wagons-lits on the <u>Sud Express</u>, from Irun, at Lisbon Santa Apolonia. Since wires had not reached Porto, railcars avoided engine change.

First glimpse of steam: as seen from the <u>Lusitania </u>Express from Madrid,
an Alco 2-8-2 of 1945, one of 22 such engines, on a mixed train east of Entroncamento.

On the main line at Setil, north of Lisbon, #35, a Sharp-Stewart 0-6-0 of 1875. At Setil a vital connecting line
diverged, the only link between CP's northern and southern systems, otherwise kept separate by the broad
Tagus estuary until a high-level bridge was finally completed in the 1990s.

Another sighting from the <u>Lusitania</u> sleeper: 0-6-2T #027, built by Beyer-Peacock in 1891, with a 2-8-4T, at Setil. This engine is one of almost 40 saved (in varying condition).

A Henschel 4-6-0 of 1909 leading a wire train on the main line north of Coimbra-Bifurcação.

Salazar's Portugal of proud tradition, and poverty: the beach at Espinho, south of Porto, along CP's main line from Lisbon to the North.

Our journey northward also gave glimpses of rural Portugal, still a deeply traditional society, with much illiteracy away from the cities, peasants in traditional garb, and yoked oxen pulling wagons. Portugal was even poorer than Spain, especially out in the countryside—one reason for the well-filled branch-line and narrow gauge trains we'd soon photograph.

To a considerable degree this traditional way of life was deliberate: Portugal's long-time ruler (from the late 1920s), Antonio de Olivera Salazar, was committed to returning Portugal to the heroic imperial past celebrated in the national epic, Camões Lusiad. This was more than sentimental nostalgia: as a traditionalist and a trained economist (but one who did not deify free markets), Salazar saw the destabilizing potential of industry and commerce, and sought to find work for young people in the development of Portugal's overseas empire. The Franco regime in Spain had attempted something similar, but reversed course after 1957 when new professional-economist advisors warned that only a more open, consumer-oriented society could avoid continued stagnation and collapse. (A good account of Salazar's regime, written just after the revolution that ended it, is in Antonio de Figuerede's Portugal: 50 Years of Dictatorship (1976). And the Anglo-Iberian novelist Robert Wilson has written two vivid historical novels about Portugal from the 1940s to the present; the best known is A Small Death in Lisbon.)

When we visited in 1963, Salazar had five more years of active control, his regime eleven years. And Salazar had been successful in producing quite a few patriotic people, proud of the empire they were just beginning to lose their sons in defending. A waiter in Porto told me the delicious coffee was Portuguese and when I looked surprised, he said "from Angola!" with emphasis.

CP's approach to Porto: looking from the Douro road bridge at Vila Nova de Gaia, with a steam train on the CP line high on the hill, and port wine lodges along the river, including Sandeman's at right.

Steamy station: the cramped quarters of Porto São Bento as seen from the parallel street, now the 31 de Janiero. When São Bento station was opened just after 1900, destroying a Renaissance church in the process, there was relatively little demand for passenger service in this impoverished society. A century later São Bento can accommodate only suburban trains; others terminate at Campanha.

Inside São Bento: 1870s pusher for local train, ca. 1916 2-6-4T to push a Lisbon express, with new silver cars, up the grade.

Cramped quarters in the heart of the city: 85 year-old 0-6-0 and newer 2-6-4T ready to push ancient and modern trains out of São Bento.

A general view of CP's cliffside line between Porto São Bento and Campanha stations, with a commuter train being pushed up the grade, and a train of modern cars from the South easing across the 1877 Maria Pia bridge over the Douro.

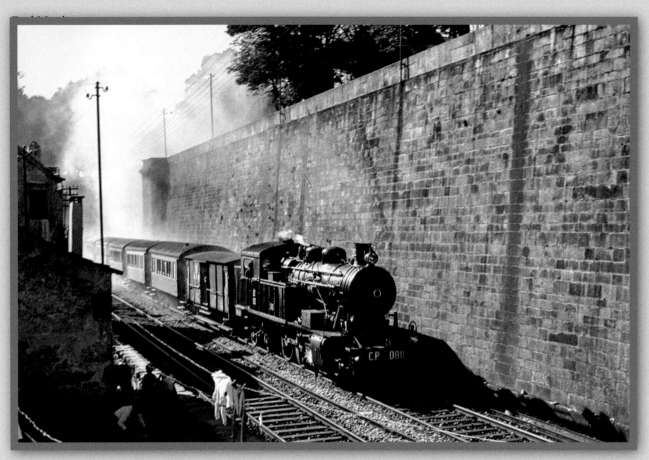

The laundry line; A German 4-6-0 blasts up the grade from Porto São Bento
to suburban Campanha.

Eight cars need a banker on the grade, with station pilot 24,
built by Beyer-Peacock in 1878, doing the job.

Class envy? #67, a Societé Alsacienne 0-6-0 of 1889, with the Campanha engine house just visible. This 0-6-0 has been preserved at Entroncamento.

Porto Campanha roundhouse, with its tiny "Mouse" shop switcher #002, built by Hartmann in Germany, in 1881, and pedestrians exercising their traditional rights.

Just north of Campanha, a gleaming German 4-6-0 of 1903 design comes off the shed to find its train, while a 2-6-4T with running-boarded coaches and old friend #24 prepare to depart for the north (or east, as the Douro valley line branches off a few miles north at Ermesinde)

Arriving in Porto, our <u>Foguete</u> reversed at Campanha and descended between cliffside houses to the cramped, atmospheric trainshed at São Bento, just clear of a tunnel mouth. Our palatial hotel, the Batalha, was on the hill above the station. From the handsome dark Edwardian room we looked over trams climbing the Rua dos Clerigos beyond São Bento, and could see steam and hear engines shunting and departing.

Porto, indeed, was in 1963 not only a uniquely picturesque city with its old quarters clinging to the cliffs above the Douro river, but a true railfan's paradise, still largely steam powered. There was frequent action on the scenic line up the cliff above the Douro between Sao Bento and "suburban" Campanha station, some distance above the north end of Eiffel's spindly Maria Pia bridge of 1877. An English visitor in the 1950s described this densely-populated urban cliff as having "a touch of China." Campanha still had a busy steam loco shed , plus a suburban service pulled by a variety of power. The ancient 0-6-0s, which preserved a sense of the mid-19th Century, added the ultimate in nostalgia.

We also regressed a few miles down the Lisbon route to the little white resort of Espinho, where the busy main line skirted the Atlantic beaches and lagoons. Here there was a surprising amount of broad-gauge activity, including ancient compartment stock with running-boards on local trains from Porto, and heavy freight trains that—especially when headed by the Alco 2-8-2s of 1945—could have been transplanted from an American railroad circa 1950. The CP broad gauge was a wonderland.

A CP local train runs along the beaches into Espinho, a small resort town south of Porto.

One of the 28 2-6-4 tanks built from 1916 to 1929 comes through the sparse suburbs of Espinho, past a French-style distant signal, pulling ancient compartment stock with running-boards for the ticket-collector.

One of the 1945 Alco-built 2-8-2s brings a longish freight north through Espinho,
with the metre-gauge terminus behind.

Leisurely switching by the Alco Mikado at Espinho.

Very broad: a handsome 221-class ten-wheeler, one of 32 from German and Belgian builders between 1903 and 1926, with 63" drivers, shunts freight at Espinho.

The later development of Portugal's railway has some bright spots, but overall is probably less encouraging than any other European country except perhaps Poland. The bright spots include a major speedup of the main Lisbon-Porto service, which has gone from 340 minutes in 1962, and 245 minutes in 1973, to 175 minutes in 2005 for the 210 miles. And modern freight services have regained a respectable volume of truck-competitive traffic on the broad gauge, much of it international. The surviving, if truncated, metre-gauge branches off the broad-gauge Douro Valley line now run some steam-powered excursion trains, though there are still closure threats. And suburban service around the two major cities has increased, as in Spain. Perhaps not least, Santiago de Calatrava's magnificent Oriente station in the Lisbon suburbs has given Portugal a great work of modern architecture.

Otherwise, the decline of "country" passenger services continues, apparently due to a government policy of building a modern consumer economy based on private motoring and massive expenditure on roads. Portugal's pro-road policy may have been derived from Spain's motorization drive after 1958, and on advice and aid from the U.S.A. But it has continued long after Spain reversed course and embarked on a massive development of high-speed rail lines. Even more, Portugal seems to be gradually closing its international passenger rail connections. There were five cross-border routes in 1963. Now we see only the two railcars between Porto and Vigo, the Sud Express to the northeast across Spain to the French border, and the Lusitania Express to Madrid, now a luxury Talgo sleeper train. Rumors circulate of the Sud's demise.

There is talk of new high-speed lines; certainly Spain would like to see much faster transborder services. The barrier seems to lie in Portugal, which faces a hard-pressed economy, with traditional industries like cork under threat, unemployment rising, and perennial budget deficits (in part due to the massive road-building programs). Perhaps this small country fears too-close integration with its confident and more prosperous neighbor. The old adage that Portugal and Spain march forward back-to-back seems even more true today. Some delightful lines, broad and narrow, do remain, making charming Portugal still worth a visit.

That Ipana smile: the sparkling face of the Portugese narrow gauge,
personified by a German-built 2-6-0T E86, of 1886, pausing briefly at Porto Trindade station.
Like most of the metre-gauge fleet, E86 has been preserved.

Chapter 3:   <u>Sparkling, Clean, and Busy: Porto's Narrow Gauge System.</u>

At Espinho, the little resort south of Porto, we had our first experience of CP's extensive metre-gauge systems (six of them). Espinho was the northwestern outpost of a hinterland-opening network, the old Vale de Vouga company, to Viseu, Santa Comba Dao, and back to Aviero on the broad-gauge south of Espinho. The first impression revealed that CP's narrow-gauge equipment was "main-line" in size, larger than that of many Spanish systems. At Espinho it could be unclear for a moment whether the fairly modern (1911-1923) metre-gauge 2-4-6-0 tanks were not on the broad gauge. The trains we saw were long and well-patronized, as was the busy system in Porto itself. We did not see the four long metre-gauge branches off the Douro Valley broad gauge; perhaps these had more of the dead-end air that Americans associated with narrow gauge. CP's metre-gauge locos were also even cleaner and more gleaming with polish than the broad-gaugers.

In Porto itself, there was a major narrow gauge system, with its own station, the six-platform Trindade, on the northern edge of the central business district, some seven blocks north of broad-gauge São Bento. Trindade was a fascinating place, surprisingly busy at the four rush hours, (including early-afternoon "siesta") with vintage Mallet tanks and 2-6-OTs pulling older coaches. In the mid-1960s thirty-five round trips were scheduled. Some modern coaches were pulled by powerful 'express' tanks built by Henschel of Germany in 1931. At peak hours it was routine to have two or three trains active within a few minutes, plus brisk switching to reposition the locomotive at the front end for speedy departure. CP in general had a reputation for brisk, confident running, as in Britain or Switzerland; Trindade exemplified this tradition. There were a few railcars, including a tiny 4-wheel charmer built to cut costs soon after the reorganized CP assumed control in 1948. But most passengers rode behind steam in a wonderful assortment of coaches of circa 1890 design, often rebuilt in local shops, plus some newer "boomers" from the obscure CF Miniero da Lena, a short-lived line of the 1920s near the monastic town of Batalha. The rebuildings and renumberings over the years have made it difficult to match the cars in my photos with the massive data in W.J.K. Davies's definitive <u>Narrow Gauge Railways of Portugal</u> ({Plateway Press, 1998)

An essential service: a midday mixed train at Espinho, south of Porto,
loading for the inland center of a separate metre-gauge division,
draws one of 18 heavy Henschel 2-4-6-0T mallets, built from 1911 into the early 1920s.

E 181 was the first of the big 2-4-6-0 compound tanks, built by Henschel in 1911. Here it starts the
heavy mixed out of Espinho, passing a 'modernismo' or Art-Nouveau façade of about the same date.

Freight car 1449 had been built for the Vale de Vouga,
the private company which built this Vouga network from 1908.

Lighter train, lighter loco: E94, a French Decauville 2-6-0T of 1910, arrives the Espinho terminus with a passenger train from Sernada. This complex Vouga system was built out from Espinho after 1908 with heavy state subsidy, to open an isolated rural area.

The little 1910 Decauville 2-6-0T at Espinho.

Mid-afternoon action at Trindade: an empty train backs out,
while a 'modern' Henschel 'express tank' 2-8-2T of 1931 arrives.

Rush hour on the urban metre-gauge: Porto Trindade, with commuters returning from the noon break and departure clocks set for the next departure. A Henschel 0-4-4-0T of 1905-08 with a new railcar, one of ten from Allan in Rotterdam in 1955.

Passengers returning to work after lunch, indifferent to both an 0-6-6-0T Mallet of 1908 and a Henschel express tank of 1931.

As the evening peak looms, a homebuilt rail bus of around 1948, built by CP to cut costs after it took over the narrow gauges, leaving on what was likely a day- tripper return out the Fafe line. These tiny cars seated 26. The very narrow steel coaches came from Italy, in 1931-2, in the project that included the Henschel 'express tanks' and the Trindade extension.

Metre-gauge modernity: Henschel 2-8-2T of 1931 cozies onto an evening train at Trindade.

Adding to Trindade's fascination was a photogenic location, with city trams passing above the smoky mouth of a tunnel that brought the narrow gauge in from the northern suburbs. The one modern note was the color-light signaling, (installed in 1938 when the Trindade extension opened) which reflected the system's importance as a heavy passenger carrier. It is fitting that in the early 21st Century its heavier lines are re-opening as an electrified light-rail network.

The Trindade system had been built between 1875 and 1948 (the last a short connecting link over broad-gauge track), originally by two small companies that later were merged into the CF Norte de Portugal. The impetus for the first narrow gauge lines was rather similar to that in Spain—local elites trying to open up resources for shipment to cities and abroad. In Portugal, however, the resources were both industrial and agricultural; the lines would allow shipment of grapes and other produce, and also bring seasonal workers out to the orchards. Beyond that, the rivers of the Minho area furnished water power, and later hydroelectric power for industry, in the small towns and cities northeast of Porto.

The first line built, the 900mm. gauge Companhia dos Caminhos de Ferro de Porto à Póvoa de Varzim e Famalicão, was more passenger-oriented, since it would serve two developed coastal resorts, Villa do Conde and Póvoa de Varzim, "Porto's northern lung." Its projectors' names suggest Anglo-Luso and German-Luso families. Opened in 1875, its original rolling stock was English; from 1889 to the last new steam power in 1931, suppliers were largely German. This line developed substantial passenger service to the resorts, and some commuter service over the first miles out of Porto Boa Vista. A cross-country extension from Póvoa to Famalicão on the broad-gauge line from Porto north to the Spanish border opened in 1881, and an industrial line was rebuilt into a branch to the new coastal port at Leixoes in 1891. (The Rio Douro, with its colorful sailing vessels, was narrow and dangerous for newer, larger steamships, so an artificial port was built along the Atlantic, to serve the busy export trade in wines.)

A separate company, the London-based CF de Guimarães, built an isolated metre-gauge line up a valley from the broad-gauge junction at Trofa to serve industry and the tourist city of Guimarães. The two companies were merged into the Norte de Portugal (under direction of the young economy minister, Salazar) in 1927, with the government helping to finance improvements: a metre-gauge connection from the Povoa line to Trofa to give Guimarães a through line to Porto; rebuilding the Póvoa line to metre-gauge; and building the long-planned extension, partly in tunnel, from a point near Boa Vista into Trindade on the edge of central Porto. Government plans had been more extensive: the Norte would have been joined to the other metre-gauge lines into a comprehensive system. But the Depression, and the growth of road traffic, ended that vision.

One of the dozen Henschel 0-4-4-0Ts takes an evening train out of Senhora da Hora on the Guimarães-Fafe line.

Vintage coaches, built to a 1905 Belgian design for the old Porto-Póvoa-Famalicão line, on the Guimarães line train just above Senhora da Hora as it turns away from the track to Póvoa.

One of the original Emil Kessler 2-6-0Ts (Esslingen, Germany, 1887) arriving in Senhora from the short Matosinhos line. Most commuter traffic was within a ten-mile zone around Porto.

Dual gauge, four rails: a train from Trindade via Trofa entering Famalicão, on the metre gauge track which diverges here, for the Atlantic Coast.

The train from Porto loads at Famalicão, before taking the hill-and-dale line over to the coast at Póvoa de Varzin. The varnished wooden coach was a real boomer, having come to CP from Portugal's most obscure narrow-gauge, the CF Miniero do Lena.

A first-class coach, Portugese-built in 1909, in service at Famalicão on a train for Porto Trindade.

A few miles west of Famalicão, E163 meets E169, both Henschel 0-6-6-0Ts.

Eagle eye: vigilance was needed at stations where people
wandered, here west of Famalicão.

E163 after arrival at Póvoa de Varzim, at the Famalicão platform.

General view at Póvoa, with E163 on the train from Famalicão at far right, the turntable, small storage and coaling area, and an Allan railcar of circa 1955 for Porto at the station. The beach is about four blocks to the left.

Busy hours over: E85 of 1887, built by Emil Kessler in Esslinger, Germany, with a train of early 20th Century coaches at Porto Trindade, after the evening's two-way rush hour. Last glimpse of a splendid system.

Porto Trindade finally opened in 1938 with colour-light signaling from the start. Although these expenditures, plus the Depression, ruined the Norte's finances, and it came under direct government control even before the CP consolidated all lines (except Lisbon-Cascais) in 1947, its policy of suburban development did work, creating the busy rush hours we witnessed in 1963. The CP built the last narrow-gauge extension, between broad-gauge rails a few miles to Famalicão to form a loop, in 1948. (There were other extensions, up the Douro, into the 1950s: Salazar's traditionalism extended to railways.)

A map of the complicated "Norte" system (not finished until after the Norte company vanished) looked like a medieval heraldic device. There was a short branch out to the harbor at Matosinhos, which turned left at Senhora da Hora, the network's hub about 2½ miles from Trindade. The busiest line ran 17 miles north to the seaside resort and commuter town of Póvoa de Varzim. Branching off northeast from Senhora da Hora was the long rural route to the historic city of Guimarães, and on to Fafe, 52 miles from Porto. At Trofa, 16 miles from Trindade, the Fafe line joined the broad-gauge main line north from Porto to the Minho region and across the border into Spain. The Guimarães trains shared the mixed-gauge for a short distance to Lousado, while a mixed-gauge section (the metre-gauge rails between the broad) to Famalicão served trains that then wandered north and west through scrub forest to Póvoa de Varzim, forming a large metre-gauge loop.

The Famalicão-to-Póvoa line rocked leisurely over light rail through new-growth forest, more in tune with the image of narrow gauge; but the commuter operation out of Porto Trindade, with its gleaming locomotives and rapid-fire operation, was a demonstration of narrow-gauge railroading at its most attractive and efficient. It's satisfying to know that it is now electrified and extended into central Porto as a light-rail system. Narrow-gauge steam continued to operate into the 1970s, and many locos remained in store thereafter. Some have now found new life in excursion service, both in Portugal and elsewhere. One of the bigger mallets is now on the Chemin de Fer du Jura in Switzerland.

Always a car in sight, or at least a tram route: an STCP Route 20 circular car passes above the busy scene at Porto Trindade station.

Chapter 4: <u>Tramways of the Northwest: Porto, Braga, Vigo.</u>

The sight of old American-style streetcars passing above the tunnel-throat at Porto Trindade reminds us of Porto's greatest attraction for trans-Atlantic enthusiasts over the last fifty years. The brown-and-cream (or white) cars of Companhia Carris de Ferro do Porto were remarkably American in appearance, since the system was electrified in the early 1900s with cars built by J.G. Brill of Philadelphia. In later years the company shops built many more units to Brill designs. Indeed, the idea of street railways was so closely associated with America that Porto's original horsecar line, in the 1870s, was called "Linha Ferrea Americana."

The city purchased the system in 1946, renaming it Transportes Colectivos do Porto (S.T.C.P.), and at the peak in the early 1950s there were 50 route miles and 93 track miles, served by some 200 motor cars and 24 trailers. Many streets in this European version of San Francisco were almost too steep for motor cars, let alone trailers. In the late 1950s trolley coaches replaced the lines across the Douro bridges to the south, and plans were formulated for very gradual conversion of the whole rail system. There seems to have been no government pressure, just the ageing of the streetcar fleet plus growing motor traffic conflicting with the wide standard-gauge cars on central Porto's steep-and-narrow streets.

When we visited in 1963 most of the system survived, and was a delight to ride and photograph. As in Lisbon, we concentrated on what turned out to be the long-term survivor—the long riverside/coastal/central loop served by an overlapping group of routes, out to the Foz do Duoro, and north above the beaches of the Praia to turn inland to Boavista, with their surviving stub north to Matosinhos of the truncated harbor line. Much of this network (Boavista to Matosinhos) had originally been a steam tramway. In recent years most of this little system-within-a-system has run as a tourist line, terminating at a traffic circle at Boavista, northwest of the city centre. As of 2006 this tourist line was in some doubt, due to new plans to operate the Avenida da Boavista as a light-rail line.

More trams in sight: looking west over the city center from the Batalha hotel, above São Bento station (in foreground), with two classic brown-and-cream cars in the Praça da Liberdade, in front of the Sandemans Port sign, and the classic streetcar street, the Rua dos Clérigos, leading up to the 18th Century Torre dos Clérigos, 246 feet high.

With the city hall looming to the North, a Porto standard, homebuilt to Brill design, crosses the Praça da Liberdade to tackle the Clérigos hill.

Contrasting architecture, contrasting trams: A homebuilt "streamliner" of c.
1950 matches the new concrete-block store, while a traditional Brill-type
car blends with the 18th Century Igreja dos Clérigos.

Another home-built "Brill" car on circular route 21 climbing into the divided street at the Clérigos church, struggling with the motor traffic that persuaded the city to opt for buses. The standard-gauge Porto cars were a tight fit on the city's narrow streets.

Beyond the Clérigos hill the old city became more gritty: a standard tram on inner-circle route 21 passing another azulejo-clad church, with trolley-coach wire making an appearance on route 3 which ran a short way west to Lordelo.

Riverside route 1 close to the center, with a Brill-type trailer of series 1-7, featuring walkover rattan seats.

Authentic American: Porto 271, built by Brill about 1912, on Avenida do Brazil in Foz do Douro,
above the river's mouth. Route 17 looped here, then headed north along the cliffs to turn
east on Boavista to downtown.

A Belgian-built 1930s car negotiates Foz do Douro on Route 1,
which ran along the Douro, then the cliffs to Matosinhos.

Along the beaches north of Foz, routes 1,2,17, and 18 gave ample service.

A Standard leaves the cut-back Matosinhos terminal, just around the corner.
The line had been truncated by the new bridge to the harbor.

Vineyard route: one of the Belgian 1930s cars on the long 9 line out to the broad-gauge rail junction at Ermesinde, northeast of Porto.

Standard 162 may have been built by Brill itself, or by Carris do Porto to the Brill design. Here it enters Ermesinde village.

Our other foray out of central Porto was on the long Route 9 to a suburban railway junction at Ermesinde (5½ miles), which clattered through vineyards on narrow, traditionally-paved and walled streets, that gave a sense of the town continuing into the countryside.. At Ermesinde, a steam local train turned up, so we hopped it for a faster ride back to São Bento.

As so often, the most photogenic part of the S.T.C.P. was in the centre, where the wide trams squeezed through narrow streets past incredibly ornate Baroque churches and almost equally decorated Edwardian office buildings. Altogether, with trams galore, broad and narrow steam, Porto was an exciting city.

Our last Portugese tramway line was infinitely small by the time of our visit, since it had closed two months earlier. We took the trip up a short CP branch off the Minho main line to the little sacred city of Braga, where a vintage tram route had run from the Estacão out to the pilgrimage church of Bom Jesus do Monte with its famous stairway to heaven. Alas, the tiny (4½ route-miles) tramway had closed at the end of May, though we were able to see the last cars parked at the barn. A harbinger of the future in Iberia, though in Portugal the decline would be gradual, and incomplete.

All too soon, it was time to take our bags down the hill to Porto's São Bento trainshed, for the 8.55 AM train to the Spanish port of Vigo, 5 hours and 109 rail miles north. Vigo had a long history: it was here that a Spanish treasure fleet from the Indies was captured and/or sunk by the British and Dutch in 1702; but its growth had come largely since 1850, especially after railways connected it to central Spain in 1885. So there was little ancient architecture.

Still, Vigo was remarkably moving to me because with its background Ria (bay) and its solid blocks of neo-Baroque commercial architecture, it gave a vivid image of what my native San Francisco looked like before the Earthquake/Fire of 1906. Since Atlantic Iberia, Porto as well as Vigo, built in traditional style well into the 20th Century, some of this ornate centre probably dated from the boom years of the Primo de Rivera dictatorship in the 1920s. Whatever, it was the perfect picture of a late-19th Century seaport city in a spectacular location.

Not least of Vigo's charms was our particular target, the brilliant white trams and interurban cars of the metre-gauge TEVCA, or Tranvias Electricos de Vigo. No trams have ever been more visible to motorists and pedestrians than Vigo's, with their sparkling white paint and silver pantographs. Like so many Spanish urban systems, the TEVCA had been opened quite late, the city network in 1914, and the coastal interurban down to Bayona, about 16 miles, in 1926. A separate company ran an 8-mile rural route east to Porrigo. The late openings are less surprising when one notes that Vigo's population in 1900 was around 18,000, though the surrounding area was fairly populous. Even in 1950 Vigo had only 50,000 people; it has grown greatly since, becoming Europe's largest fishing port.

Northern Portugal: Braga in its hills northeast of Porto, seen from the pilgrimage church of Bom Jesus.

End of the lines: Braga Municipal cars 3 and 8, built by Brill about 1914,
resting next to a motor bus also replaced by trolley coaches on May 28, 1963.

Neo-Baroque in Vigo: Car 26 of Vigo's TEVCA local system in the center
on route 3 to Victoria. The 13-mile local system used these little cars
from opening in 1914 to enforced closure in 1968.

Cyclists' friend: car 26 climbs up from historic Vigo Bay, passing below the solanas, the glassed-in balconies that Galicia uses to protect against Atlantic gales.

A half grand-union in a small city: an interurban train led by car 109 has passed one of the tiny local cars.

Light and bright: Tranvias Electricos de Vigo's paint scheme, including silver pantographs, offered ultimate visibility. The big interurbans came in the early 1920s for two long rural routes.

View flats: two Vigo local cars near Peniche, and the carhouse, along the Atlantic shore.

A Bayona train near the end of street running in Vigo.

A southbound Bayona (Baiona) train with the Peninsula de Morrazo, north of Vigo Bay, in the background. This coastwise line to beach resorts ran every 24 minutes, taking 73 minutes for about 16 miles. Someone called it "Iberia's Manx Electric."

A perfect day at Bayona. The big motors sometimes pulled 4-wheel freight cars as well as passenger trailers.

As in the rest of Spain, but more dramatically, TEVCA's demise was sudden: in 1968 its license was revoked and its cars forced off the streets. TEVCA had wanted to continue operating, but the municipality demanded buses immediately. Since city governments under Franco were not very independent, direction from Madrid seems a likelihood. Because TEVCA continued its legal existence, the brilliant white cars rotted away in storage for years. Once again the theme of coercion from Madrid is prominent: no wonder that regional autonomy movements have been so strong in Galicia, as elsewhere in Spain.

All this was unknowable in 1963, when the well-maintained, if a bit creaky, trams seemed as natural a facet of the city as the neo-baroque centre. So we enjoyed, and photographed, especially the lines out to the Atlantic coast, and then the single-track line to Bayona (now Baiona, in Gallego), with its big centre-door motors pulling similar trailers, which they ran around at the terminal.

With its light rail and many curves, the Bayona line was not fast—73 minutes end-to-end, or about 13 mph average, a train every 24 minutes. Nor were the cars especially comfortable. But they had real interurban dignity, and the Atlantic views more than compensated. Indeed, this well-patronized line, which Mike Bent, in Narrow Gauge Rails Through the Cordillera (Chichester, England: Semaphore Press, 1998), called Iberia's Manx Electric, certainly one of the world's most scenic, provided a satisfying conclusion to our exhausting, and all-too-limited tour of a Peninsula overflowing with traditional railway interest along with its better-known history and architecture.

The benevolent haze of memory: Iberia, 1963, a little Vigo local route along the Atlantic Ocean.

Printed in the United States
By Bookmasters